THE HAWTHORN SERIES

Classic Essential

∿ ❖ ∿

Chocolate

Your Promise of Success

Welcome to the world of Confident Cooking, created for you in our test
kitchen, where recipes are double-tested by our team of home
economists to achieve a high standard of success.

～ Chocolate Essentials ～

Cooking with chocolate is an art. Once perfected, it will be appreciated by all those who sample your chocolate masterpieces. Follow these hints and tips, and chocolate catastrophes will be a thing of the past.

Types of Chocolate

Dark chocolate contains sugar, cocoa liquor and cocoa butter. Types of dark chocolate include bittersweet, containing less sugar than regular dark chocolate; and semi-sweet, which can be substituted with bittersweet if a little more sugar is added to the recipe.

Milk chocolate contains the same ingredients as dark chocolate, with the addition of milk solids.

White chocolate contains sugar, full-cream milk or milk solids, cocoa butter and flavourings. It is not a true chocolate, as it contains no cocoa liquor.

Couverture chocolate is the best chocolate available. It is very high in cocoa fat, and melts and coats easily.

Compound chocolate is more economical to use than couverture chocolate. It has added vegetable fats, which allow it to set very quickly, and at room temperature. Chocolate melts, chocolate bits and chocolate chips (dark,

milk and white) are all compound chocolate.

Cocoa powder is ground from the dried, pressed remains of cocoa liquor, from which most of the cocoa butter has been removed. Dutched cocoa powder has a darker, richer colour and more mellow flavour than regular cocoa due to further processing.

Melting Chocolate

Try to melt the chocolate uniformly without burning it. Chocolate from a block should be chopped or grated into even-sized pieces for even melting. White chocolate melts better when it is grated or finely chopped. Once the chocolate has melted, work quickly before it sets. Prevent any water or steam from coming into contact with the melted chocolate. Even a small amount of liquid may cause

the chocolate to seize, rendering it unusable. If this happens—the chocolate becomes a mealy, stiff substance— you can sometimes rescue it by adding 1 tablespoon of cream or vegetable oil. If the chocolate burns, you will need to start again with fresh chocolate. Do not try to speed up the melting process.

Conventional Method
Put the chopped chocolate in a heatproof bowl. Half fill a saucepan with water and bring it to the boil. Remove from the heat and place the bowl of chocolate over the pan, making sure it is not touching the water. Stir occasionally until the chocolate is melted.

Microwave Method
Chop the chocolate into
small pieces and place in
a microwave-safe bowl.
Cook in 30-second
bursts on Medium
(50%), stirring
frequently. Chocolate
holds its shape when
melted in the
microwave, so it may
retain its squares—
check if it has melted by
stirring. Don't be
tempted to try to cook it
faster on a high heat, as
it burns easily.

Storing Chocolate
Most chocolate,
depending on its quality,
will keep for several
months. Wrap in foil or
plastic wrap, and store in
a cool, dry place.
Sometimes chocolate
will develop a white
'bloom' on its surface.
This is usually the result
of a radical temperature
change. It may occur on
chocolate that has been
overheated or on
chocolate that has been
refrigerated. The bloom
is harmless, however,
and doesn't affect the
flavour of the chocolate.
Stale chocolate can also
develop a bloom. It is
unpleasant and dry, and
should be discarded.

Hints
• Grate chocolate
quickly with a vegetable
peeler or in a food
processor and use it to
decorate the tops or
sides of cakes.

• Couverture chocolate
is the best type of
chocolate to use for
decorating, especially
fancy designs, as it sets
firmly and holds its
shape at room
temperature. Compound
chocolate can also be
used successfully.
• If chocolate is too
thick to use as a coating,
stir in a small amount of
vegetable oil or melt a
small amount of Copha
(white vegetable
shortening) and stir it
into the chocolate.
• Before coating food
with chocolate, ensure it
is free from moisture,
which will seize the
chocolate and make it
useless. After dipping,
place the food on a lined
tray and allow it to set at
room temperature.

Paper Piping Bags
To make a paper piping
bag, cut a 25 cm
(10 inch) square of
baking paper. Fold it in
half diagonally to form a
triangle. Working with
the longest side closest
to you, curl the left point
in to meet the top point.

Hold in place while
wrapping the other side
around tightly to form a
cone shape. Secure with
tape or a staple. Tuck

the upstanding ends into
the cone. Fill with the
melted chocolate and
fold the top edges to
seal. Snip off the tip and
gently apply pressure
from the top of the bag.

～ Chocolate Mud Cake ～

Preparation time:
20 minutes
Total cooking time:
2¹/4 hours
Serves 8

1¹/2 cups (185 g/6 oz)
self-raising flour
¹/2 cup (60 g/2 oz) plain
flour
¹/3 cup (40 g/1¹/4 oz)
cocoa powder
250 g (8 oz) butter,
chopped
1 tablespoon oil
200 g (6¹/2 oz) dark
chocolate, chopped

1¹/2 cups (375 g/12 oz)
caster sugar
1 tablespoon instant
coffee powder
2 eggs, lightly beaten

Chocolate Topping
150 g (5 oz) butter,
chopped
150 g (5 oz) dark
chocolate, chopped

1～Preheat the oven to warm 160°C (315°F/ Gas 2–3). Grease a deep 20 cm (8 inch) round cake tin. Line the tin with baking paper. Sift the flours and cocoa powder into a large mixing bowl and make a well in the centre.
2～Combine the butter, oil, chocolate, sugar and coffee powder with 1 cup (250 ml/8 fl oz) water in a pan. Stir over low heat until the chocolate and butter are melted, and the sugar is dissolved. Remove from the heat. Pour the chocolate mixture into the well in the dry ingredients. Whisk until

just combined. Add the eggs and mix well, but do not overbeat.
3～Pour the mixture into the tin and bake for 2 hours, or until a skewer comes out clean when inserted into the centre of the cake. Leave in the tin to cool completely, then turn out onto a wire rack.
4～To make the topping, combine the butter and chocolate in a pan. Stir over low heat until the butter and chocolate are melted.

Remove from the heat and allow the mixture to cool slightly.
5～Trim the top of the cake so it will sit flat, then place it upside down on a wire rack over a baking tray. Pour the topping over the cake and allow it to run down the side. This is delicious served with crème fraîche.

NUTRITION PER SERVE
Protein 8 g; Fat 60 g; Carbohydrate 100 g; Dietary Fibre 2 g; Cholesterol 170 mg; 3880 kJ (925 cal)

Sift the flours and cocoa into a large mixing bowl.

Stir the butter, oil, chocolate, sugar, coffee powder and water until melted and smooth.

Whisk the chocolate mixture into the well in the dry ingredients.

Pour the cooled chocolate topping over the upside down cake.

～ Chocolate Mousse ～

Preparation time:
20 minutes
+ 2 hours chilling
Total cooking time:
5 minutes
Serves 4

250 g (8 oz) dark
  chocolate, chopped
3 eggs
1/4 cup (60 g/2 oz) caster
  sugar
2 teaspoons dark rum
1 cup (250 ml/8 fl oz)
  cream, softly whipped

1 ～ Put the chocolate in a heatproof bowl. Half fill a saucepan with water and bring to the boil. Remove from the heat and place the bowl over the pan, making sure it is not touching the water. Stir occasionally until the chocolate is melted. Set aside to cool.

2 ～ Using an electric mixer, beat the eggs and sugar in a small bowl for 5 minutes, or until thick, pale and increased in volume.

3 ～ Beat in the melted chocolate and the rum, then transfer the mixture to a large mixing bowl. Using a large metal spoon, gently fold in the cream until the mixture is just combined.

4 ～ Spoon the mousse into four 1 cup (250 ml/8 fl oz) dessert glasses. Refrigerate for 2 hours, or until set. Decorate with chocolate leaves (see page 55).

NUTRITION PER SERVE
Protein 9 g; Fat 50 g;
Carbohydrate 60 g; Dietary
Fibre 1 g; Cholesterol 220 mg;
2900 kJ (685 cal)

Place the chocolate over the pan, and stir occasionally until it is melted.

Beat the eggs and sugar until they are thick, pale and increased in volume.

Beat the chocolate and rum into the egg and sugar mixture.

Transfer the mixture to a large bowl and fold in the cream until just combined.

～ Chocolate Choc-chip Cookies ～

Preparation time:
20 minutes
Total cooking time:
15 minutes
Makes about 25

1¹/₂ cups (185 g/6 oz) plain flour	150 g (5 oz) dark chocolate, chopped
³/₄ cup (90 g/3 oz) cocoa powder	3 eggs, lightly beaten
1¹/₂ cups (345 g/11 oz) firmly packed soft brown sugar	1 cup (175 g/6 oz) dark chocolate bits
180 g (6 oz) butter	¹/₂ cup (90 g/3 oz) white chocolate bits

1 ～Preheat the oven to moderate 180°C (350°F/Gas 4). Grease 2 baking trays and line with baking paper. Sift the flour and cocoa into a bowl. Add the sugar.
2 ～Combine the butter and dark chocolate in a pan. Stir over low heat until melted, then add to the flour mixture with the eggs and stir until combined. Stir in all the chocolate bits.
3 ～Roll 2 level tablespoons of the mixture into balls. Place on the trays, allowing room for spreading. Flatten slightly, then bake for 12 minutes. Leave for 5 minutes, then cool on a wire rack.

NUTRITION PER COOKIE
Protein 3 g; Fat 10 g; Carbohydrate 30 g; Dietary Fibre 1 g; Cholesterol 40 mg; 830 kJ (200 cal)

Sift the flour and cocoa powder into a mixing bowl.

Stir the butter and dark chocolate over low heat with a wooden spoon.

Pour the melted chocolate into the sifted flour mixture.

Roll the mixture into rough balls, place on the trays and flatten the cookies slightly.

∼ Chocolate Sauces ∼

These sauces make a delicious dessert when drizzled over anything from ice cream to puddings to fruit, but it is difficult to resist the temptation of eating them by the spoonful.

Dark Chocolate Sauce

Put 150 g (5 oz) chopped dark chocolate in a bowl. Bring 300 ml (10 fl oz) cream to the boil in a pan. Stir in 2 tablespoons caster sugar, then pour it over the chocolate. Leave for 2 minutes, then stir until smooth. Add a spoonful of any liqueur. Serve warm. Makes 375 ml (12 fl oz)

NUTRITION PER SERVE (6)
Protein 2 g; Fat 30 g; Carbohydrate 25 g; Dietary Fibre 0 g; Cholesterol 70 mg; 1500 kJ (360 cal)

Vanilla Hazelnut Sauce

Put 300 ml (10 fl oz) cream in a pan. Split 1 vanilla pod lengthways and scrape the seeds into the cream. Add the pod and bring to the boil. Remove from the heat, cover and leave for 10 minutes, then strain. Put 200 g ($6^1/2$ oz) finely chopped white chocolate in a bowl, reheat the cream and pour it over the chocolate. Leave for 2 minutes, then stir until melted. Stir in $^1/4$ cup (30 g/1 oz) chopped

roasted hazelnuts. Serve warm. Makes 430 ml (14 fl oz)

NUTRITION PER SERVE (7)
Protein 4 g; Fat 30 g; Carbohydrate 20 g; Dietary Fibre 1 g; Cholesterol 60 mg; 1440 kJ (340 cal)

Caramel Bar Sauce

Chop 4 Snickers bars. Place $^1/4$ cup (60 ml/ 2 fl oz) milk and $^3/4$ cup (185 ml/6 fl oz) cream in a small pan. Add the Snickers bars and stir over low heat until the chocolate and caramel have melted. Add 100 g

Left to right: Dark Chocolate Sauce; Vanilla Hazelnut Sauce; Caramel Bar Sauce; Choco-latte Sauce; Jaffa Sauce

(3^1/$_2$ oz) chopped milk chocolate and stir until melted. Cool to room temperature. Makes 500 ml (16 fl oz)

NUTRITION PER SERVE (8)
Protein 2 g; Fat 15 g; Carbohydrate 9 g; Dietary Fibre 0 g; Cholesterol 35 mg; 675 kJ (160 cal)

Choco-latte Sauce

Put 100 g (3^1/$_2$ oz) chopped dark chocolate in a bowl. Combine 100 g (3^1/$_2$ oz) chopped unsalted butter, ^{1}/$_2$ cup (125 g/4 oz) caster sugar, 300 ml (10 fl oz) cream, ^{1}/$_3$ cup (40 g/ 1^1/$_4$ oz) cocoa powder and 2 tablespoons freshly ground coffee in a pan. Bring to the boil, then simmer, stirring, for 2 minutes. Strain the mixture over the chocolate and leave for 2 minutes, then stir until melted. Serve warm. Makes 500 ml (16 fl oz)

NUTRITION PER SERVE (8)
Protein 3 g; Fat 30 g; Carbohydrate 30 g; Dietary Fibre 0 g; Cholesterol 80 mg; 1600 kJ (380 cal)

Jaffa Sauce

Cut 3 large strips of peel from an orange, avoiding the white pith. Heat in a small pan with ^{1}/$_2$ cup (125 ml/4 fl oz) orange juice. Bring to the boil, then stir in 2 tablespoons caster sugar. Simmer for about 3 minutes, or until thick and syrupy, and reduced to 2 tablespoons. Cool, then cut the rind into thin strips. Put 200 g (6^1/$_2$ oz) chopped milk chocolate in a bowl. Bring 300 ml (10 fl oz) cream to the boil, then pour it over the chocolate and leave for 2 minutes. Stir until melted, then stir in the orange syrup, rind and 2 teaspoons Cointreau. Serve warm. Makes 500 ml (16 fl oz)

NUTRITION PER SERVE (8)
Protein 3 g; Fat 25 g; Carbohydrate 25 g; Dietary Fibre 0 g; Cholesterol 60 mg; 1290 kJ (305 cal)

~ Black Forest Gateau ~

Preparation time:
45 minutes
Total cooking time:
15 minutes
Serves 8

¹/₃ cup (40 g/1¹/₄ oz) plain flour	3¹/₂ cups (875 ml/ 28 fl oz) cream, whipped
¹/₃ cup (40 g/1¹/₄ oz) self-raising flour	700 g (1 lb 6 oz) jar morello cherries or
2 tablespoons cocoa powder	2 x 425 g (14 oz) cans pitted dark cherries, well drained (see Notes)
4 eggs, separated	250 g (8 oz) block dark chocolate
¹/₂ cup (125 g/4 oz) caster sugar	maraschino cherries, to garnish
¹/₄ cup (60 ml/2 fl oz) Kirsch (see Notes)	icing sugar, to dust

1 ~ Preheat the oven to moderate 180°C (350°F/ Gas 4). Grease two shallow 20 cm (8 inch) round sandwich tins and line with baking paper. Sift the flours and cocoa onto greaseproof paper 3 times.

2 ~ Place the egg whites in a small, clean, dry mixing bowl. Using an electric mixer, beat until firm peaks form. Add the sugar gradually, beating constantly until the sugar has dissolved and the mixture is thick and glossy. Add the yolks and beat for 20 seconds. Transfer the mixture to a larger bowl.

3 ~ Fold in the flours and cocoa quickly and lightly in 2–3 batches. Spread the mixture evenly into the tins and bake for 15 minutes, or until the cakes are springy to the touch. Leave them in the tins for 5 minutes before turning out onto wire racks to cool. Cut each cake in half horizontally.

4 ~ Brush the top of one round of cake with some of the Kirsch. Spread with a layer of the whipped cream and top with one third of the cherries. Place another round of cake on top. Repeat brushing with the Kirsch and layering with the cream and cherries, finishing with the last round of cake. Using a flat-bladed knife, cover the cake completely with the cream, reserving some for decoration.

5 ~ Using a vegetable peeler, shave curls from the edge of the block of chocolate. Press some of the chocolate curls lightly onto the cream around the side of the cake. Decorate the top of the cake with rosettes of the reserved whipped cream and the maraschino cherries. Pile some more chocolate curls in the centre of the cream and cherries, and dust the cake with icing sugar.

NUTRITION PER SERVE
Protein 10 g; Fat 60 g; Carbohydrate 50 g; Dietary Fibre 3 g; Cholesterol 240 mg; 3265 kJ (780 cal)

Notes ~ Kirsch is a cherry-flavoured liqueur. Black Forest Gateau is traditionally prepared using fresh morello cherries, poached in a sugar syrup and pitted. Bottled morello cherries or canned, pitted cherries are a good substitute. Drain the cherries well on paper towels to prevent the colour from staining the whipped cream.

Using a large, serrated knife, cut the cakes in half horizontally.

Brush the cakes with the Kirsch and layer with the whipped cream and cherries.

～ Rich Chocolate Truffles ～

Preparation time:
40 minutes
+ overnight chilling
Total cooking time:
10 minutes
Makes about 30

3/4 cup (185 ml/6 fl oz) thick cream	70 g (2¼ oz) butter, chopped
400 g (13 oz) dark chocolate, grated	2 tablespoons Cointreau dark cocoa powder, for rolling

1～Place the cream in a small pan and bring to the boil. Remove from the heat and stir in the chocolate until it is completely melted. Add the butter and stir until the butter is melted. Stir in the Cointreau. Place in a large bowl, cover and refrigerate for several hours or overnight, or until firm enough to roll.

2～Quickly roll tablespoons of the mixture into balls, and refrigerate until firm.

Roll the balls in the cocoa. Shake off any excess and return to the refrigerator. Serve at room temperature.

NUTRITION PER TRUFFLE
Protein 1 g; Fat 9 g;
Carbohydrate 9 g; Dietary
Fibre 0 g; Cholesterol 15 mg;
500 kJ (120 cal)

～ Rum-and-raisin Truffles ～

Preparation time:
30 minutes + soaking
and chilling
Total cooking time:
5 minutes
Makes about 40

1/2 cup (60 g/2 oz) raisins, finely chopped	1 teaspoon ground cinnamon
1/4 cup (60 ml/2 fl oz) rum	1/2 cup (50 g/1¾ oz) pecans, finely chopped
200 g (6½ oz) chocolate-coated wheatmeal biscuits, crushed	1/4 cup (60 ml/2 fl oz) cream
1/3 cup (60 g/2 oz) lightly packed soft brown sugar	250 g (8 oz) dark chocolate, chopped
	1/4 cup (90 g/3 oz) golden syrup
	1¼ cups (125 g/4 oz) pecans, finely ground

1～Combine the raisins with the rum, cover and marinate for 1 hour. Put the biscuits, sugar, cinnamon and pecans in a large mixing bowl. Mix until combined.

2～Place the cream, chocolate and golden syrup in a pan. Stir over low heat until melted. Pour onto the biscuit mixture with the raisin mixture. Stir until well combined. Refrigerate until just firm enough to roll into balls.

3～Roll tablespoons of the mixture into balls, then roll in the pecans. Refrigerate until firm.

NUTRITION PER TRUFFLE
Protein 1 g; Fat 7 g;
Carbohydrate 10 g; Dietary
Fibre 1 g; Cholesterol 3 mg;
470 kJ (110 cal)

Rich Chocolate Truffles (top) and Rum-and-raisin Truffles

～ Baked Chocolate Cheesecake ～

Preparation time:
20 minutes
+ overnight chilling
Total cooking time:
1 hour
Serves 8–10

125 g (4 oz) plain chocolate biscuits	500 g (1 lb) cream cheese, softened
1/4 cup (40 g/1 1/4 oz) chopped toasted almonds	1/2 cup (115 g/4 oz) firmly packed soft brown sugar
90 g (3 oz) butter, melted	1/2 cup (125 ml/4 fl oz) cream
1 tablespoon soft brown sugar	2 eggs, beaten
1 cup (250 ml/8 fl oz) cream, whipped	1 teaspoon grated orange rind

Filling
125 g (4 oz) dark chocolate, chopped

Candied Orange Slices
1 1/4 cups (310 g/10 oz) sugar
2 oranges, thinly sliced

1 ～ Grease a 20 cm (8 inch) round springform tin and line the base with baking paper. Put the biscuits in a food processor with the almonds and process into crumbs. Add the butter and sugar, and process until well combined. Press firmly over the base of the tin. Refrigerate until firm. Preheat the oven to warm 160°C (315°F/Gas 2–3).
2 ～ To make the filling, put the chocolate in a heatproof bowl. Half fill a pan with water and bring to the boil. Remove from the heat and place the bowl over the pan, making sure it is not touching the water. Stir occasionally until melted. Cool slightly. Beat the cream cheese and sugar until creamy. Blend in the cooled chocolate, cream, eggs and rind, and mix until smooth. Pour the filling over the base and smooth the surface.

Place the tin on a baking tray and bake for 50–55 minutes, or until the filling is firm. Leave to cool in the tin, then refrigerate overnight.
3 ～ To make the candied orange slices, combine 1 cup (250 g/ 8 oz) of the sugar with 1/3 cup (80 ml/2 3/4 fl oz) water in a pan. Stir over low heat, without boiling, until the sugar dissolves. Bring to the boil, then reduce the heat and add half the orange slices to the syrup. Cook for about 15–20 minutes, or until the orange slices are transparent and toffee-like. Remove from the syrup and allow to cool on a tray lined with baking paper. Add the

remaining sugar to the syrup and stir gently to dissolve—the juice from the fruit will break down the concentrated syrup and the fruit won't candy properly unless you add more sugar. Cook the remaining orange slices, then remove from the syrup and cool on the tray.
4 ～ Decorate the cheesecake with the whipped cream and the candied orange slices.

NUTRITION PER SERVE (10)
Protein 9 g; Fat 50 g; Carbohydrate 60 g; Dietary Fibre 1 g; Cholesterol 160 mg; 2940 kJ (700 cal)

Note ～ Alternatively, the cheesecake may be decorated with fresh segments of orange.

Use the back of a spoon to press the biscuit mixture firmly over the base of the tin.

Pour the mixture over the base and smooth the surface.

～ Petits Pots au Chocolat ～

Preparation time:
20 minutes
+ 6–8 hours chilling
Total cooking time:
1 hour
Serves 8

---

^{2}/3 cup (170 ml/
  5^1/2 fl oz) thick cream
^{1}/2 vanilla pod, split
  lengthways
150 g (5 oz) dark
  bittersweet chocolate,
  chopped
^{1}/3 cup (80 ml/2^3/4 fl oz)
  milk
2 egg yolks
^{1}/4 cup (60 g/2 oz)
  caster sugar
whipped cream and
  cocoa powder, to
  serve

1～Lightly brush eight ^{1}/3 cup (80 ml/2^3/4 fl oz) capacity ramekin pots with melted butter. Place the pots in a deep baking dish. Preheat the oven to very slow 140°C (275°F/Gas 1).

2～Place the cream in a small pan with the split vanilla pod. Heat until the cream is warm, then remove from the heat and leave the vanilla pod to infuse.

3～Combine the chocolate and milk in a small pan. Stir over low heat until the chocolate has just melted.

4～Place the egg yolks in a small mixing bowl and slowly stir in the sugar. Continue stirring until the sugar has dissolved and the mixture is light in colour. Scrape the seeds out of the vanilla pod into the cream and discard the empty pod. Add the vanilla cream and the melted chocolate mixture to the beaten egg yolks, and mix until well combined.

5～Pour the mixture into the ramekin pots, filling approximately two-thirds full. Fill the baking dish with enough boiling water to come halfway up the sides of the pots. Bake for 45 minutes, or until the chocolate pots have puffed up slightly and feel spongy. Remove from the baking dish and cool completely. Cover with plastic wrap and refrigerate for 6–8 hours before serving. Serve chilled, with a dollop of cream and a sprinkle of sifted cocoa powder.

NUTRITION PER SERVE
Protein 2 g; Fat 15 g; Carbohydrate 25 g; Dietary Fibre 0 g; Cholesterol 75 mg; 1020 kJ (245 cal)

Note～The pots will have a slight crust on the top when they first come out of the oven.

Scrape the seeds out of the vanilla pod and discard the empty pod.

Pour the mixture into the ramekin pots, filling them two thirds of the way.

~ Sacher Torte ~

Preparation time:
40 minutes
Total cooking time:
1 hour
Serves 10

1 cup (125 g/4 oz) plain
 flour
1/4 cup (30 g/1 oz) cocoa
 powder
1 cup (250 g/8 oz) caster
 sugar
100 g (3 1/2 oz) butter
1/4 cup (80 g/2 3/4 oz)
 strawberry jam
4 eggs, separated

Ganache Topping
2/3 cup (170 ml/5 1/2 fl oz)
 cream
200 g (6 1/2 oz) dark
 chocolate, chopped
1/3 cup (90 g/3 oz) caster
 sugar

1 ~ Preheat the oven to moderate 180°C (350°F/ Gas 4). Grease a deep 20 cm (8 inch) round cake tin, line with baking paper and grease the paper.

2 ~ Sift the flour and cocoa into a large bowl. Make a well in the centre. Combine the sugar, butter and half the jam in a small pan. Stir over low heat until the butter is melted and the sugar has dissolved, then add to the flour mixture with the egg yolks and stir until just combined.

3 ~ Beat the egg whites with an electric mixer until soft peaks form. Stir a third of the egg white into the cake mixture, then fold in the remainder in 2 batches. Pour into the tin and smooth the surface. Bake for 40–45 minutes, or until a skewer comes out clean when inserted into the centre. Leave in the tin for 15 minutes before turning onto a wire rack.

4 ~ To make the topping, stir the cream, chocolate and sugar over low heat until the mixture is melted and smooth. If the mixture begins to separate, stir in 1 tablespoon water.

5 ~ Level the top of the cake, then turn it upside down on a wire rack over a tray. Melt the remaining jam and brush it over the cake. Pour most of the topping over the cake and tap the tray to flatten the surface. Place the remaining mixture in a piping bag and pipe 'Sacher' on the top of the cake.

NUTRITION PER SERVE
Protein 6 g; Fat 25 g; Carbohydrate 60 g; Dietary Fibre 1 g; Cholesterol 120 mg; 1990 kJ (475 cal)

Stir the sugar, butter and half the jam over low heat.

Stir the butter mixture and the egg yolks into the flour mixture.

Fold the remaining egg white into the mixture with a metal spoon.

Tap the tray on the bench to flatten the surface of the topping.

～ Rum-and-raisin Ice Cream ～

Preparation time:
1 hour + soaking and
overnight freezing
Total cooking time:
30 minutes
Serves 4

---

1 tablespoon rum
1/2 cup (60 g/2 oz)
  raisins, finely
  chopped
8 egg yolks
1/2 cup (125 g/4 oz)
  caster sugar
2 tablespoons cocoa
  powder
2 cups (500 ml/16 fl oz)
  milk
1 cup (250 ml/8 fl oz)
  cream
1 vanilla pod, split
  lengthways
250 g (8 oz) dark
  chocolate, chopped

1～Combine the rum
and raisins in a bowl,
cover and marinate for
1 hour.
2～Place the egg yolks
in a medium heatproof
bowl and gradually
whisk in the sugar.
Continue to whisk until
the sugar has dissolved
and the mixture is light
and creamy. (Do not use
an electric mixer as this
will incorporate too

much air into the
mixture.) Stir in the
sifted cocoa.
3～Place the milk and
cream in a pan. Scrape
the seeds from the
vanilla pod into the pan
and add the pod. Bring
to the boil, then remove
from the heat and
remove the vanilla pod.
Gently whisk the hot
milk into the egg-yolk
mixture. Place the bowl
over a pan of simmering
water, making sure it
does not touch the
water, and stir over low
heat until the custard
lightly coats the back of
a spoon. This will take
about 20 minutes. Do
not allow the mixture
to boil. Remove the
custard from the heat
and strain into a clean
bowl. Place a deep
20 cm (8 inch) square
cake tin in the freezer.
4～Put the chocolate in
a heatproof bowl. Half
fill a saucepan with
water and bring to the
boil. Remove from the
heat and place the bowl
over the pan, making
sure it is not touching
the water. Stir
occasionally until the
chocolate is melted. Add
the warm chocolate to
the warm custard and
stir constantly until the

chocolate is mixed
through. Stir in the rum
and raisin mixture, and
allow to cool. Pour the
cooled mixture into the
chilled container, cover
with foil and freeze until
the ice cream is just set.
5～Remove the ice
cream from the freezer
and spoon it into a large
bowl. Beat with an
electric mixer until
smooth and thick, then
return to the container,
cover and freeze
overnight, or.until set. If
the ice cream is very
hard, put it in the
refrigerator for
15–20 minutes before
serving for it to soften.

NUTRITION PER SERVE
Protein 15 g; Fat 60 g;
Carbohydrate 90 g; Dietary
Fibre 2 g; Cholesterol 460 mg;
4030 kJ (965 cal)

Note～If you don't
have time to soak the
raisins for 1 hour, place
the rum and raisins in a
small microwave-safe
container. Cover and
cook on Medium (50%)
for 1 minute, or until
hot. Remove from the
microwave and leave
until cold.
Variation～Substitute
brandy and dried
apricots for the rum and
raisins in this recipe.

Stir the custard over simmering water until it lightly coats the back of a wooden spoon.

When the ice cream has just set, transfer it to a bowl and beat until smooth and thick.

～ Chocolate Clusters ～

Preparation time:
25 minutes
Total cooking time:
10 minutes
Makes about 40

125 g (4 oz) dark chocolate melts	125 g (4 oz) glacé ginger, chopped
125 g (4 oz) white chocolate melts	30 g (1 oz) each dark chocolate and white chocolate melts, extra, melted
2/3 cup (125 g/4 oz) dried mixed fruit	

1～Put the dark chocolate in a heatproof bowl. Half fill a pan with water and bring it to the boil. Remove from the heat and place the bowl over the pan, making sure it is not touching the water. Stir until melted. Allow to cool slightly. Repeat with the white chocolate.
2～Stir the mixed fruit into the dark chocolate. Combine the ginger with the white chocolate.
3～Drop spoonfuls of the mixtures onto foil-lined trays, and leave to set at room temperature. Drizzle with the extra melted chocolate.

NUTRITION PER CLUSTER
Protein 1 g; Fat 2 g; Carbohydrate 7 g; Dietary Fibre 0 g; Cholesterol 1 mg; 205 kJ (50 cal)

～ Chocolate-coffee Cups ～

Preparation time:
40 minutes
Total cooking time:
10 minutes
Makes 20

200 g (6½ oz) dark chocolate melts	50 g (1¾ oz) white chocolate, chopped
20 foil cups	1 tablespoon Tia Maria
1 tablespoon cream	10 coffee beans, halved

1～Put the dark chocolate in a heatproof bowl. Half fill a pan with water and bring to the boil. Remove from the heat and place the bowl over the pan, making sure it is not touching the water. Stir occasionally until melted. Cool slightly.
2～Working with one at a time, put 1 teaspoon of chocolate in each cup. Use a small paintbrush to coat the inside with chocolate, making sure it is thick and there are no gaps. Turn the cups upside down on a wire rack and leave until firm. Set the remaining chocolate aside.
3～Combine the cream, white chocolate and Tia Maria in a heatproof bowl. Stir over a pan of simmering water until smooth. Cool slightly, then spoon into the chocolate cups. Press half a coffee bean into each cup. Allow to set.
4～Remelt the reserved chocolate. Spoon it over the filling, and tap gently to level the surface. Leave to set.

NUTRITION PER CUP
Protein 1 g; Fat 4 g; Carbohydrate 8 g; Dietary Fibre 0 g; Cholesterol 2 mg; 285 kJ (70 cal)

Chocolate Clusters (top) and Chocolate-coffee Cups

～ Chocolate Hazelnut Pudding ～

Preparation time:
25 minutes
Total cooking time:
2 hours
Serves 6

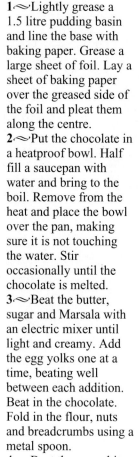

1～Lightly grease a
1.5 litre pudding basin
and line the base with
baking paper. Grease a
large sheet of foil. Lay a
sheet of baking paper
over the greased side of
the foil and pleat them
along the centre.
2～Put the chocolate in
a heatproof bowl. Half
fill a saucepan with
water and bring to the
boil. Remove from the
heat and place the bowl
over the pan, making
sure it is not touching
the water. Stir
occasionally until the
chocolate is melted.
3～Beat the butter,
sugar and Marsala with
an electric mixer until
light and creamy. Add
the egg yolks one at a
time, beating well
between each addition.
Beat in the chocolate.
Fold in the flour, nuts
and breadcrumbs using a
metal spoon.
4～Beat the egg whites
with an electric mixer
until soft peaks form.
Gradually beat in the

125 g (4 oz) dark chocolate, chopped 100 g (3½ oz) butter ⅓ cup (90 g/3 oz) caster sugar 2 tablespoons Marsala 4 eggs, separated ½ cup (60 g/2 oz) plain flour ¾ cup (80 g/2¾ oz) ground hazelnuts	½ cup (40 g/1¼ oz) stale breadcrumbs ¼ cup (60 g/2 oz) caster sugar, extra icing sugar, to dust *Mascarpone Cream* 150 g (5 oz) dark chocolate, chopped 250 g (8 oz) mascarpone, at room temperature 2 tablespoons Marsala

extra sugar, 1 tablespoon
at a time, making sure it
has dissolved before the
next addition. Beat until
thick and glossy. Stir a
spoonful of the egg-
white mixture into the
chocolate mixture using
a large metal spoon.
Carefully fold in the
remaining egg white
until just combined.
5～Spoon the mixture
into the basin and cover
with the foil and paper,
foil-side-up. Place the
lid over the foil and
secure the clips. If you
don't have a lid, secure
the foil with string under
the lip of the basin.
Make a handle from the
string by tying a double
length of string to either
side of the string around
the edge of the basin.
6～Place the basin on
an upturned saucer in a
large, deep pan. Pour

boiling water down the
side of the pan to come
halfway up the side of
the basin. Bring to the
boil, then reduce the
heat slightly and
simmer, covered, for
1¾ hours, or until a
skewer inserted into the
centre comes out clean.
Leave the pudding for
5 minutes before turning
out. Dust with the icing
sugar and serve with the
mascarpone cream.
7～To make the
mascarpone cream, melt
the chocolate as in
step 2, then allow it to
cool slightly. Gently
soften the mascarpone
with a spoon or whisk,
and gradually mix in the
Marsala and chocolate.

NUTRITION PER SERVE
Protein 15 g; Fat 50 g;
Carbohydrate 100 g; Dietary
Fibre 3 g; Cholesterol 165 mg;
3760 kJ (900 cal)

Using a large metal spoon, fold the egg-white mixture into the chocolate mixture.

Cover the basin with the pleated foil and paper, foil-side-up.

～ Chocolate Swiss Roll ～

Preparation time:
25 minutes
+ 30 minutes chilling
Total cooking time:
12 minutes
Serves 6–8

---

3 eggs
1/2 cup (125 g/4 oz)
  caster sugar
1/4 cup (30 g/1 oz) plain
  flour
2 tablespoons cocoa
  powder
1 cup (250 ml/8 fl oz)
  cream
1 tablespoon icing
  sugar
1/2 teaspoon vanilla
  essence

1～Preheat the oven to moderately hot 200°F (400°F/Gas 6). Lightly grease the base and sides of a 23 x 30 cm (9 x 12 inch) swiss roll tin. Line the base with paper and grease the paper. Place the eggs in a small bowl with 1/3 cup (90 g/3 oz) of the caster sugar. Beat with electric beaters for about 8 minutes, or until the mixture is thick and creamy.

2～Sift the flour and cocoa together and gently fold into the egg mixture with a metal spoon. Spread the mixture evenly into the prepared tin.

3～Bake for about 12 minutes, or until the cake is just set. Meanwhile, place a clean tea towel on a work surface, top with a sheet of baking paper and sprinkle with the remaining caster sugar. When the cake is cooked, turn it out immediately onto the prepared paper and sugar. Roll the cake up from the long side, rolling the paper inside the roll and using the tea towel as a guide. Stand the rolled cake on a wire cake rack for 5 minutes, then carefully unroll the cake and allow it to cool to room temperature.

4～Beat the cream, icing sugar and vanilla essence until stiff peaks form. Spread the cream over the cooled cake, leaving a 1 cm (1/2 inch) border around each edge. Reroll the cake, using the paper as a guide. Place the roll, seam-side-down, on a tray. Refrigerate, covered, for 30 minutes. Dust the top of the swiss roll with icing sugar before cutting into slices to serve.

NUTRITION PER SERVE (8)
Protein 4 g; Fat 15 g; Carbohydrate 20 g; Dietary Fibre 0 g; Cholesterol 110 mg; 1025 kJ (245 cal)

Beat the eggs and sugar with electric beaters until thick and creamy.

Gently fold the sifted flour and cocoa into the egg mixture.

Turn the roll out onto the prepared paper
and roll up from the long side.

Spread the cream over the roll and reroll,
using the paper as a guide.

～ Chocolate Drinks ～

Chocolate was originally consumed by the Aztecs in the form of a bitter, unsweetened drink. These chocolate treats may be in the same form as their ancient ancestor, but are far superior in taste.

Iced Strawberry Chocolate Whip

Stir 50 g ($1^3/4$ oz) chopped dark chocolate and $1/4$ cup (60 ml/ 2 fl oz) milk over low heat until melted. Stir in $1/2$ cup (125 ml/4 fl oz) milk and refrigerate until cold. Process 60 g (2 oz) strawberries with 2 teaspoons icing sugar, a large scoop of vanilla ice cream and the chocolate milk in a food processor or blender until smooth. Serves 1

NUTRITION PER SERVE
Protein 10 g; Fat 25 g; Carbohydrate 50 g; Dietary Fibre 2 g; Cholesterol 30 mg; 1915 kJ (460 cal)

Clockwise, from left: Iced Strawberry Chocolate Whip; Iced Mocha Thickshake; Iced Chocolate; Banana and Chocolate Smoothie; Hot Chocolate; Orange Whisky Cream

Iced Mocha Thickshake

Put 2 tablespoons rich chocolate topping, 2 scoops chocolate ice cream, $1/4$ cup (60 ml/ 2 fl oz) cold strong coffee and $1/4$ cup (60 ml/2 fl oz) cold milk in a blender. Blend until thick and creamy, adding more milk if the mixture is too thick. Top with whipped cream and decorate with chocolate shavings. Serves 1

NUTRITION PER SERVE
Protein 5 g; Fat 15 g; Carbohydrate 35 g; Dietary Fibre 0 g; Cholesterol 50 mg; 1210 kJ (290 cal)

Iced Chocolate

Pour 2 tablespoons rich chocolate topping into a glass. Swirl it around the sides, then three-quarters fill with icy-cold milk. Add a scoop of vanilla ice cream and a big swirl of whipped cream. Dust with drinking chocolate. Serves 1

NUTRITION PER SERVE
Protein 8 g; Fat 20 g; Carbohydrate 35 g; Dietary Fibre 0 g; Cholesterol 60 mg; 1370 kJ (330 cal)

Banana and Chocolate Smoothie

Combine 2 scoops chocolate ice cream, 1 chopped banana and $^1/_2$ cup (125 ml/4 fl oz) milk in a blender, and blend until smooth and creamy. Dip the edge of a tall glass in egg white, then dip in finely grated chocolate. Pour in the smoothie. Serves 1

NUTRITION PER SERVE
Protein 10 g; Fat 15 g; Carbohydrate 45 g; Dietary Fibre 3 g; Cholesterol 30 mg; 1430 kJ (340 cal)

Hot Chocolate

Heat 1 cup (250 ml/ 8 fl oz) milk in a pan. Mix in $1^1/_2$ tablespoons drinking chocolate. Put 2 marshmallows in a tall mug. Pour in the hot chocolate and serve topped with chocolate shavings. Serves 1

NUTRITION PER SERVE
Protein 10 g; Fat 10 g; Carbohydrate 35 g; Dietary Fibre 0 g; Cholesterol 35 mg; 1290 kJ (305 cal)

Orange Whisky Cream

Put $^1/_2$ cup (125 ml/ 4 fl oz) milk, $^1/_4$ cup (60 g/2 oz) caster sugar and $1^1/_2$ tablespoons drinking chocolate in a pan. Stir over low heat until the sugar dissolves. Cool, then stir in $^1/_2$ cup (125 ml/4 fl oz) cream and 2 tablespoons Grand Marnier. Refrigerate until chilled. Serves 2

NUTRITION PER SERVE
Protein 4 g; Fat 30 g; Carbohydrate 55 g; Dietary Fibre 0 g; Cholesterol 95 mg; 2200 kJ (525 cal)

～ White Chocolate Puffs ～ with Dark Chocolate Sauce

Preparation time:
40 minutes + cooling
Total cooking time:
50 minutes
Serves 4–6

60 g (2 oz) butter
³/₄ cup (90 g/3 oz) plain
    flour
3 eggs, lightly beaten

White Chocolate Filling
¹/₄ cup (30 g/1 oz)
    custard powder
1 tablespoon caster
    sugar
1¹/₂ cups (375 ml/
    12 fl oz) milk
150 g (5 oz) white
    chocolate melts,
    chopped
1 tablespoon Grand
    Marnier

Dark Chocolate Sauce
125 g (4 oz) dark
    chocolate, chopped
¹/₂ cup (125 ml/4 fl oz)
    cream

1～Preheat the oven to hot 210°C (415°F/ Gas 6–7). Line a baking tray with baking paper. Put the butter and ³/₄ cup (185 ml/6 fl oz) water in a pan. Bring to the boil, then remove from the heat. Add the flour all at once. Return to the heat and stir until the mixture forms a smooth ball. Set aside to cool slightly. Transfer the mixture to a bowl and, while beating with an electric mixer, gradually add the eggs, beating well after each addition, to form a smooth, glossy paste.
2～Spoon 2 heaped teaspoons of the mixture onto the tray at 5 cm (2 inch) intervals. Sprinkle with water and bake for 10 minutes. Reduce the heat to moderate 180°C (350°F/ Gas 4) and bake for 12–15 minutes, or until the dough is puffed. Cut a slit in the base of each puff, turn off the oven and leave them to dry in the oven for 5 minutes.
3～To make the filling, combine the custard powder and sugar in a pan. Gradually add the milk, stirring until smooth, then continue to stir over low heat until the mixture boils and thickens. Remove from the heat and add the white chocolate and Grand Marnier. Stir until the chocolate is melted. Cover the surface with plastic wrap and allow to cool. Stir the custard until smooth, then spoon into a piping bag fitted with a 1 cm (¹/₂ inch) plain nozzle. Pipe the filling into each puff. Serve with the warm chocolate sauce.
4～To make the chocolate sauce, combine the chocolate and cream in a pan. Stir over low heat until the chocolate is melted and the mixture is smooth. Serve warm.

NUTRITION PER SERVE **(6)**
Protein 10 g; Fat 35 g;
Carbohydrate 50 g; Dietary
Fibre 1 g; Cholesterol 160 mg;
2265 kJ (540 cal)

Notes～The puffs can be made a day ahead. Fill just before serving. You can also make miniature puffs for an alternative to after-dinner chocolates. Make the puffs with 1 teaspoon of the mixture. Dip the tops of the cooked puffs in melted chocolate. Allow to set, then fill with whipped cream.

Add the flour, then stir over the heat until the mixture forms a smooth ball.

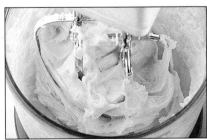

Gradually beat in the eggs to form a smooth, glossy paste.

～ Best-ever Chocolate Cake ～

Preparation time:
25 minutes
Total cooking time:
50 minutes
Serves 10

125 g (4 oz) butter
1/2 cup (125 g/4 oz)
  caster sugar
1/3 cup (40 g/1 1/4 oz)
  icing sugar, sifted
2 eggs, lightly beaten
1 teaspoon vanilla
  essence
1/4 cup (80 g/2 3/4 oz)
  blackberry jam
1 1/4 cups (155 g/5 oz)
  self-raising flour
1/2 cup (60 g/2 oz) cocoa
  powder

1 teaspoon bicarbonate
  of soda
1 cup (250 ml/8 fl oz)
  milk

Chocolate Butter Cream
50 g (1 3/4 oz) dark
  chocolate, finely
  chopped
25 g (3/4 oz) butter
3 teaspoons cream
1/4 cup (30 g/1 oz) icing
  sugar, sifted

1 ～ Preheat the oven to moderate 180°C (350°F/ Gas 4). Grease the base and sides of a deep 20 cm (8 inch) square cake tin, and line with baking paper.
2 ～ Beat the butter, caster sugar and icing sugar with an electric mixer in a small mixing bowl until the mixture is light and creamy. Add the eggs gradually, beating thoroughly between each addition. Add the vanilla and jam, and beat until combined.
3 ～ Transfer the mixture to a large mixing bowl. Using a metal spoon, fold in the combined sifted flour, cocoa and bicarbonate of soda alternately with the milk. Stir until the mixture is just combined and almost smooth.
4 ～ Pour into the tin and smooth the surface. Bake for 45 minutes, or until a skewer comes out clean when inserted into the centre of the cake. Leave in the tin for 15 minutes before cooling on a wire rack.
5 ～ To make the butter cream, combine the chopped chocolate, butter, cream and icing sugar in a small pan. Stir over low heat until the mixture is smooth and glossy. Spread the butter cream over the top of the cake using a flat-bladed knife.

NUTRITION PER SERVE
Protein 5 g; Fat 20 g; Carbohydrate 40 g; Dietary Fibre 1 g; Cholesterol 85 mg; 1495 kJ (360 cal)

Beat the butter and sugars in a small bowl until light and creamy.

Fold in the sifted flour, cocoa and soda alternately with the milk.

Pour the mixture into the paper-lined tin and smooth the surface.

Stir the chocolate, butter, cream and icing sugar until smooth and glossy.

~ Chocolate Caramel Slice ~

Preparation time:
30 minutes + cooling
Total cooking time:
40 minutes
Makes about 18 pieces

Coconut Base
1 cup (125 g/4 oz) self-
raising flour
1 cup (90 g/3 oz)
desiccated coconut
1/2 cup (125 g/4 oz)
caster sugar
125 g (4 oz) butter,
melted

Caramel Filling
20 g (3/4 oz) butter
2 tablespoons golden
syrup
400 g (13 oz) sweetened
condensed milk

Chocolate Topping
150 g (5 oz) dark
chocolate, chopped
20 g (3/4 oz) Copha
(white vegetable
shortening)

---

1. ~ Preheat the oven to moderate 180°C (350°F/ Gas 4). Grease an 18 x 28 x 3 cm (7 x 11 x 1¼ inch) tin. Line the base and 2 sides of the tin with baking paper.

2. ~ To make the base, sift the flour into a bowl. Mix in the coconut and sugar. Stir in the butter, then press firmly into the tin. Bake for 15–20 minutes, or until golden. Gently press the base with the back of a spoon to level the surface. Allow to cool.

3. ~ To make the filling, put the butter, golden syrup and condensed milk in a small pan. Stir constantly over low heat for 5–10 minutes, or until lightly caramelized. Immediately pour the filling over the base and spread evenly. Bake for 10 minutes. Allow the slice to set and cool.

4. ~ To make the topping, put the chopped chocolate and Copha in a heatproof bowl. Half fill a saucepan with water and bring to the boil. Remove from the heat and place the bowl over the pan, making sure it is not touching the water. Stir until the mixture is melted and smooth, then spread it over the caramel filling using a metal spatula. Refrigerate to set the chocolate. Remove from the tin and cut into slices with a hot, dry knife.

NUTRITION PER PIECE
Protein 3 g; Fat 15 g; Carbohydrate 30 g; Dietary Fibre 1 g; Cholesterol 30 mg; 1150 kJ (275 cal)

Gently press the cooked base with the back of a spoon to give a level surface.

Stir the butter, golden syrup and condensed milk until lightly caramelized.

Place the chocolate and Copha over the pan, and stir until melted and smooth.

Spread the chocolate topping over the caramel filling with a metal spatula.

∼ Chocolate Peppermint Creams ∼

Preparation time:
40 minutes + chilling
Total cooking time:
20 minutes
Makes about 40

---

65 g (2¼ oz) butter
¼ cup (60 g/2 oz) caster
  sugar
½ cup (60 g/2 oz) plain
  flour
⅓ cup (40 g/1¼ oz) self-
  raising flour
2 tablespoons cocoa
  powder
2 tablespoons milk

Peppermint Cream
1 egg white
1¾ cups (215 g/7 oz)
  icing sugar, sifted
2–3 drops peppermint
  essence or oil, to taste

Chocolate Topping
150 g (5 oz) dark
  chocolate, chopped
150 g (5 oz) dark
  chocolate melts

1∼Preheat the oven to moderate 180°C (350°F/ Gas 4). Line 2 baking trays with baking paper. Using an electric mixer, beat the butter and sugar in a small bowl until light and creamy. Transfer to a medium bowl. Add the sifted flours and cocoa alternately with the milk. Mix with a knife until the mixture forms a soft dough. Turn out onto a floured surface and gather together into a rough ball.

2∼Cut the dough in half. Roll each half between 2 sheets of baking paper to a 2 mm (⅛ inch) thickness. Slide onto a tray and refrigerate for 10–15 minutes, or until firm. Cut the dough into rounds using a 4 cm (1½ inch) plain round cutter, rerolling the scraps of dough and cutting out more rounds. Place the rounds on the trays, allowing room for spreading. Bake for 10 minutes. Transfer the biscuits to a wire rack to cool completely.

3∼To make the peppermint cream, place the egg white in a small bowl. Using an electric mixer, beat in the icing sugar, 2 tablespoons at a time, on low speed. Add more icing sugar, if necessary, until a soft dough forms.

4∼Turn the dough onto a surface dusted with icing sugar and knead in enough icing sugar so that the dough is not sticky. Knead in the peppermint essence.

5∼Roll a teaspoon of peppermint cream into a ball, and flatten slightly. Sandwich between 2 chocolate biscuits, pressing together to spread the peppermint to the edges. Repeat with the remaining filling and chocolate biscuits, keeping the filling covered as you work.

6∼To make the topping, put the chopped chocolate and the chocolate melts in a heatproof bowl. Half fill a saucepan with water and bring to the boil. Remove from the heat and place the bowl over the pan, making sure it is not touching the water. Stir occasionally until the chocolate is melted. Remove from the heat and allow to cool slightly. Use a fork to dip the biscuits into the chocolate and allow any excess to drain away. Place on a baking paper-lined tray to set.

NUTRITION PER BISCUIT
Protein 1 g; Fat 4 g; Carbohydrate 15 g; Dietary Fibre 0 g; Cholesterol 4 mg; 375 kJ (90 cal)

Sandwich the filling between 2 biscuits, pressing to spread it to the edges.

Use a fork to dip the biscuits into the melted chocolate.

∼ Chocolate Hazelnut Torte ∼

Preparation time:
1 hour
+ overnight chilling
Total cooking time:
1 1/4 hours
Serves 10

---

500 g (1 lb) dark
  chocolate, chopped
6 eggs
2 tablespoons
  Frangelico (see Note)
1 1/2 cups (165 g/5 1/2 oz)
  ground hazelnuts
1 cup (250 ml/8 fl oz)
  cream, whipped
12 whole hazelnuts

Chocolate Topping
200 g (6 1/2 oz) dark
  chocolate, chopped
3/4 cup (185 ml/6 fl oz)
  cream
1 tablespoon
  Frangelico

---

1 ∼ Preheat the oven to slow 150°C (300°F/ Gas 2). Grease a deep 20 cm (8 inch) round cake tin and line with baking paper.

2 ∼ Put the chocolate in a heatproof bowl. Half fill a saucepan with water and bring to the boil. Remove from the heat and place the bowl over the pan, making sure it is not touching the water. Stir occasionally until the chocolate is melted.

3 ∼ Put the eggs in a large heatproof bowl and add the Frangelico. Place the bowl over a pan of barely simmering water over low heat, making sure it does not touch the water. Beat with an electric mixer on high speed for 7 minutes, or until the mixture is light and foamy. Remove from the heat.

4 ∼ Using a metal spoon, quickly and lightly fold the melted chocolate and ground nuts into the egg mixture until just combined. Fold in the cream and pour the mixture into the tin. Place the tin in a shallow baking dish. Pour in enough hot water to come halfway up the side of the tin.

5 ∼ Bake for 1 hour, or until just set. Remove the tin from the baking dish. Cool to room temperature, cover with plastic wrap and refrigerate overnight.

6 ∼ Cut a 17 cm (6 3/4 inch) circle from heavy cardboard. Invert the chilled cake onto the disc so that the base of the cake becomes the top. Place on a wire rack over a baking tray and remove the baking paper. Return the cake to room temperature before decorating.

7 ∼ To make the topping, combine the chopped chocolate, cream and Frangelico in a small pan. Heat gently over low heat, stirring, until the chocolate is melted and the mixture is smooth.

8 ∼ Pour the chocolate mixture over the cake in the centre, tilting slightly to cover the cake evenly. Tap the baking tray gently on the bench so that the top is level and the icing runs completely down the side of the cake. Place the hazelnuts around the edge of the cake. Refrigerate just until the topping has set and the cake is firm. Carefully transfer the cake to a serving plate, and cut into wedges to serve.

NUTRITION PER SERVE
Protein 9 g; Fat 50 g; Carbohydrate 50 g; Dietary Fibre 1 g; Cholesterol 180 mg; 2650 kJ (630 cal)

Note ∼ Frangelico is a hazelnut-flavoured liqueur. Brandy or whisky may also be used.

Quickly and lightly fold the chocolate and nuts into the egg mixture.

Stir the chocolate, cream and Frangelico over low heat until the mixture is smooth.

～ Rich Chocolate Muffins ～

Preparation time:
25 minutes
Total cooking time:
20 minutes
Makes 12

2¹/₂ cups (310 g/10 oz) self-raising flour	3 eggs, lightly beaten
1 tablespoon cocoa powder	chocolate curls, to decorate (see page 55)
200 g (6¹/₂ oz) dark chocolate, chopped	icing sugar, to dust
150 g (5 oz) butter, chopped	*Chocolate Icing*
3/4 cup (140 g/4¹/₂ oz) lightly packed dark brown sugar	1 cup (125 g/4 oz) icing sugar
	¹/4 cup (30 g/1 oz) cocoa powder
¹/₂ cup (125 ml/4 fl oz) milk	50 g (1³/4 oz) butter, softened
	2 tablespoons milk

1 ～Preheat the oven to moderately hot 200°C (400°F/Gas 6). Grease a medium 12-hole muffin tin. Sift the flour and cocoa into a large mixing bowl.

2 ～Combine the chocolate and butter in a small pan. Stir constantly over low heat until the chocolate and butter are melted. Add the brown sugar and stir to combine.

3 ～Add the chocolate mixture to the dry ingredients with the milk and eggs. Mix with a large metal spoon until just combined. Do not overmix—the batter should look quite lumpy. Spoon the mixture into the muffin tin, filling each hole about three-quarters full. Bake for 12–15 minutes, or until the muffins are just cooked. A skewer inserted into the centre of the muffins should come out clean. Leave the muffins in the pan for 5 minutes before turning onto a wire rack to cool.

4 ～To make the icing, sift the icing sugar and cocoa powder into a bowl. Add the softened butter and enough milk to form a thick paste. Stir until smooth, then spread the icing thickly over the muffins. Decorate with the chocolate curls and sprinkle with the sifted icing sugar.

NUTRITION PER MUFFIN
Protein 6 g; Fat 20 g; Carbohydrate 50 g; Dietary Fibre 1 g; Cholesterol 90 mg; 1740 kJ (415 cal)

Stir the chocolate and butter over low heat until they are melted.

Mix the chocolate mixture with the dry ingredients, milk and eggs.

～ Chocolate Bavarian ～

Preparation time:
30 minutes + chilling
Total cooking time:
5 minutes
Serves 6

200 g (6½ oz) dark chocolate, chopped	**⅓ cup (90 g/3 oz) caster sugar**
1½ cups (375 ml/ 12 fl oz) milk	**1 tablespoon gelatine**
4 egg yolks	**300 ml (10 fl oz) cream**

1～Combine the chocolate and milk in a small pan. Stir over low heat until the chocolate is melted and the milk just comes to the boil. Remove from the heat.
2～Beat the egg yolks and sugar with an electric mixer until thick and creamy. Gradually add the chocolate milk, beating until combined.
3～Soften the gelatine in 2 tablespoons water in a bowl over simmering water. Stir until dissolved, then stir into the chocolate mixture.
4～Refrigerate until the mixture is cold but not set, stirring occasionally. Beat the cream until soft peaks form. Fold it into the chocolate mixture in 2 batches. Pour into six 1 cup (250 ml/8 fl oz) glasses and refrigerate for several hours or overnight, until set.

NUTRITION PER SERVE
Protein 8 g; Fat 40 g; Carbohydrate 40 g; Dietary Fibre 0 g; Cholesterol 195 mg; 2140 kJ (510 cal)

Stir the chocolate and milk until the milk just comes to the boil.

Beat the egg yolks and sugar until the mixture is thick and creamy.

Soften the gelatine in 2 tablespoons water over a pan of simmering water.

Fold the softly whipped cream into the chocolate mixture in batches.

~ Rocky Road ~

Preparation time:
20 minutes + chilling
Total cooking time:
5 minutes
Makes about 30 pieces

250 g (8 oz) pink and
white marshmallows,
halved
1 cup (160 g/5¹/2 oz)
unsalted peanuts,
roughly chopped

¹/2 cup (105 g/3¹/2 oz)
glacé cherries, halved
1 cup (60 g/2 oz)
shredded coconut
350 g (11 oz) dark
chocolate, chopped

1. Line the base and 2 opposite sides of a shallow 20 cm (8 inch) square cake tin with foil. Place the marshmallows, peanuts, cherries and coconut in a bowl. Mix until well combined.
2. Put the chocolate in a heatproof bowl. Half fill a saucepan with water and bring to the boil. Remove from the heat and place the bowl over the pan, making sure it is not touching the water. Stir occasionally until the chocolate is melted.
3. Add the chocolate to the marshmallow mixture, and mix until well combined. Spoon into the tin and press evenly over the base. Refrigerate for several hours, or until set. Lift out of the tin and cut into small pieces. Store in an airtight container in the refrigerator.

NUTRITION PER PIECE
Protein 2 g; Fat 6 g;
Carbohydrate 8 g; Dietary
Fibre 1 g; Cholesterol 0 mg;
435 kJ (215 cal)

~ Chocolate-mallow Fudge ~

Preparation time:
20 minutes
+ overnight chilling
Total cooking time:
10 minutes
Makes about 40 pieces

70 g (2¹/4 oz) butter,
chopped
150 g (5 oz) dark
chocolate, chopped
250 g (8 oz) white
marshmallows

1 teaspoon vanilla
essence
50 g (1³/4 oz) milk
chocolate, melted

1. Line the base and 2 opposite sides of an 8 x 26 cm (3 x 10¹/2 inch) bar tin with foil. Place the chopped butter, chocolate and marshmallows in a pan. Stir constantly over low heat until the chocolate and marshmallows are melted. Remove from the heat and stir in the vanilla essence.
2. Pour the mixture into the tin and refrigerate for several hours or overnight, until firm. Remove the fudge from the tin and remove the foil. Cut into 2 cm (³/4 inch) slices, then cut each slice into 3 pieces. Drizzle the fudge with the melted chocolate.

NUTRITION PER PIECE
Protein 0 g; Fat 3 g;
Carbohydrate 3 g; Dietary
Fibre 0 g; Cholesterol 5 mg;
180 kJ (125 cal)

Rocky Road (top) and Chocolate-mallow Fudge

~ Chocolate Orange Tart ~

Preparation time:
45 minutes
+ 20 minutes chilling
Total cooking time:
50 minutes
Serves 6

½ cup (60 g/2 oz) plain
  flour
2 tablespoons rice flour
¼ cup (45 g/1½ oz)
  ground almonds
1 tablespoon caster
  sugar
90 g (3 oz) butter,
  chopped
1 egg yolk
whipped cream, to
  serve

Filling
100 g (3½ oz) dark
  chocolate, chopped

125 g (4 oz) milk
  chocolate, chopped
1 teaspoon grated
  orange rind
2 tablespoons orange
  juice
¾ cup (185 ml/6 fl oz)
  cream
2 eggs
2 egg yolks, lightly
  beaten

Candied Orange Rind
⅓ cup (90 g/3 oz) sugar
rind of 3 oranges,
  shredded

1 ~ Preheat the oven to moderate 180°C (350°F/ Gas 4). Lightly grease a 22 cm (8¾ inch) loose-bottomed flan tin. Place the flours, almonds, sugar and chopped butter in a large bowl. Rub the butter in until the mixture is crumbly. Add the egg yolk and 2–3 teaspoons water, or enough to just combine the ingredients. Gather the mixture together into a ball. Roll the pastry out between 2 sheets of baking paper until it is large enough to line the base and side of the tin. Refrigerate the pastry for 20 minutes, then trim the edges with a knife.

2 ~ Cut a sheet of greaseproof paper large enough to cover the tin. Lay the paper over the pastry and spread with dried beans or rice. Bake for 15 minutes, then discard the beans and paper, and bake for a further 5 minutes.

3 ~ To make the filling, put the dark and milk chocolate in a heatproof bowl. Half fill a saucepan with water and bring to the boil. Remove from the heat and place the bowl over the pan, making sure it is not touching the water. Stir occasionally until the chocolate is melted. Remove from the pan. Whisk the orange rind, juice, cream, eggs and egg yolks until combined. Gradually add to the chocolate, whisking constantly. Pour into the pastry and bake for 20–25 minutes, or until just set. (The filling will set more as it cools.)

4 ~ To make the candied orange rind, put the sugar in a pan with 2 tablespoons water. Stir over low heat until dissolved. Add the rind, bring to the boil, then reduce the heat and simmer for 5 minutes. Stir until the mixture crystallizes, then remove the rind from the syrup and allow it to cool on a sheet of baking paper. If the rind will not crystallize, sprinkle it with a little sugar while stirring the syrup.

5 ~ Serve the tart warm or cold, topped with the whipped cream and candied orange rind.

NUTRITION PER SERVE
Protein 10 g; Fat 45 g; Carbohydrate 60 g; Dietary Fibre 2 g; Cholesterol 205 mg; 2740 kJ (255 cal)

Line the base and side of the tin with the pastry, then refrigerate for 20 minutes.

Gradually whisk the cream mixture into the melted chocolate, whisking constantly.

~ Moist Chocolate Brownies ~

Preparation time:
20 minutes
Total cooking time:
50 minutes
Makes 36 squares

1½ cups (185 g/6 oz)
  plain flour
¼ cup (30 g/1 oz) cocoa
  powder
1 teaspoon baking
  powder
½ teaspoon bicarbonate
  of soda
1½ cups (205 g/6½ oz)
  chopped roasted
  macadamia nuts
125 g (4 oz) butter

200 g (6½ oz) dark
  chocolate, chopped
1 cup (250 g/8 oz) caster
  sugar
2 eggs, lightly beaten
⅓ cup (90 g/3 oz) sour
  cream

Chocolate Topping
150 g (5 oz) dark
  chocolate, chopped
½ cup (125 g/4 oz) sour
  cream

1 ~ Preheat the oven to moderate 180°C (350°F/ Gas 4). Grease a shallow 23 cm (9 inch) square cake tin. Line the base and sides with baking paper.
2 ~ Sift the flour, cocoa, baking powder and bicarbonate of soda into a large mixing bowl. Stir in 1 cup (135 g/4½ oz) of the nuts and make a well in the centre.
3 ~ Place the butter and chocolate in a heatproof bowl. Stand the bowl over a pan of simmering water, making sure it is not touching the water, and stir until the chocolate is melted and the mixture is smooth. Remove from the heat and add the sugar, eggs and sour cream. Beat with a wire whisk until the ingredients are well combined and smooth. Add the chocolate mixture to the well in the dry ingredients. Using a wooden spoon, stir until well combined, but do not overbeat.

Spread the mixture into the tin. Bake for 30–35 minutes, or until a skewer comes out clean when inserted into the centre. Cool the brownies in the tin.
4 ~ To make the topping, put the chopped chocolate in a heatproof bowl. Half fill a saucepan with water and bring to the boil. Remove from the heat and place the bowl over the pan, making sure it is not touching the water. Stir occasionally until the chocolate is melted. Remove the bowl from the pan and leave for 2 minutes. Add the sour cream and beat with a wire whisk until the mixture is thick and glossy. Spread the topping over the cooled brownies and sprinkle

with the remaining macadamia nuts. Allow the topping to set before cutting the brownies into squares.

NUTRITION PER SQUARE
Protein 2 g; Fat 15 g; Carbohydrate 17 g; Dietary Fibre 1 g; Cholesterol 25 mg; 795 kJ (190 cal)

Note ~ The brownies may be stored in an airtight container for up to 2 days or frozen, un-iced, for 1 month.
Variations ~ Use pecans or walnuts in place of the macadamia nuts. Or turn the brownies into a delicious dessert by cutting into slightly larger squares and serving warm, sprinkled with icing sugar and topped with thick cream or a scoop of ice cream.

Pour the chocolate mixture into the well in the dry ingredients and stir to combine.

Beat the melted chocolate with the sour cream until the mixture is thick and glossy.

~ Self-saucing ~ Chocolate Pudding

Preparation time:
25 minutes
Total cooking time:
40 minutes
Serves 4–6

1 cup (125 g/4 oz) self-raising flour	1 teaspoon vanilla essence
1/3 cup (40 g/1 1/4 oz) cocoa powder	icing sugar, to dust
1 1/4 cups (310 g/10 oz) caster sugar	*Orange Cream*
1/2 cup (125 ml/4 fl oz) milk	300 ml (10 fl oz) cream
1 egg	1 teaspoon grated orange rind
60 g (2 oz) butter, melted	1 tablespoon icing sugar
	1 tablespoon Grand Marnier

1 ~ Preheat the oven to moderate 180°C (350°F/Gas 4), and grease a deep 2 litre capacity ovenproof dish. Sift the flour and 2 tablespoons of the cocoa into a large mixing bowl. Stir in 1/2 cup (125 g/4 oz) of the sugar, and make a well in the centre.

2 ~ Pour in the combined milk, egg, butter and vanilla. Stir until smooth, but do not overbeat. Pour into the dish and dissolve the remaining cocoa and sugar in 2 1/2 cups (600 ml/20 fl oz) boiling water. Pour gently over the back of a spoon onto the pudding mixture.

3 ~ Bake the pudding for 40 minutes, or until a skewer comes out clean when inserted into the cake. Meanwhile, make the orange cream.

4 ~ To make the orange cream, put the cream, orange rind, icing sugar and Grand Marnier in a bowl. Using electric beaters, beat until soft peaks form.

5 ~ Dust the top of the pudding with sifted icing sugar and serve with the orange cream.

NUTRITION PER SERVE (6)
Protein 6 g; Fat 30 g; Carbohydrate 80 g; Dietary Fibre 1 g; Cholesterol 125 mg; 2550 kJ (610 cal)

Note ~ Serve the pudding immediately as it will absorb the sauce on standing.

Pour the combined milk, egg, butter and vanilla into the well in the dry ingredients.

Gently pour the cocoa mixture over the back of a spoon onto the pudding mixture.

~ Chocolate Garnishes ~

When making chocolate garnishes, use a compound chocolate.
It will be hard when it sets, due to the addition of vegetable
fats, and will keep its shape if the weather is warm.

Boxes

Cover a flat baking tray with plastic wrap or cellophane, ensuring it is free from creases. Melt 200 g (6^1/$_2$ oz) of chocolate. Spread over the plastic in a 3 mm (^{1}/$_8$ inch) layer. Leave until nearly set, then cut into even-sized squares. Allow to set. Re-melt the leftover chocolate and spread it on the edges to join the squares together to form boxes. Fill with fruit, mousse or custard. Makes 4

Dipping Strawberries

Lightly brush 250 g (8 oz) strawberries with a dry pastry brush—do not wash. Melt 150 g (5 oz) dark chocolate in a small bowl and dip each strawberry halfway into the chocolate. Allow any excess to drip off, then place on a sheet of greaseproof paper until set. Dip the tips of the strawberries in 100 g (3^1/$_2$ oz) melted white chocolate. If the chocolate is too thick, thin it with a little melted Copha (white vegetable shortening).

Left to right: Boxes; Dipping Strawberries; Cake Collar; Curls; Leaves; Sheets

Cake Collar
Melt 100 g (3¹/2 oz) dark chocolate melts. Cut a strip of baking paper that is the same width and 5 mm (¹/4 inch) longer than needed to wrap around the cake you wish to decorate. Spread the chocolate evenly over the paper and, before the chocolate sets, wrap it carefully around the cake. When set, gently peel away the paper. For a different result, cut the edges of the paper in decorative patterns. Alternatively, dot melted white chocolate onto the paper, allow to set, then spread with the dark chocolate and continue as above. Enough for a 20 cm (8 inch) round cake.

Curls
Spread 100 g (3¹/2 oz) melted dark chocolate in a thin layer on a flat piece of marble. Allow to just set. While holding a knife towards you at a 45° angle, gently drag the knife in a downward sideways motion to form chocolate curls.

Leaves
Choose 10 firm, clean, dry leaves, free from blemishes and sprays. Use rose or ivy leaves, or any non-toxic leaves. Melt 100 g (3¹/2 oz) chocolate. Using a small, clean paintbrush, brush a layer of melted chocolate over the underside of the leaf. When set, repeat with another thin layer of chocolate. Allow to set, then carefully peel away the leaf. Makes about 10

Sheets
Cover a flat baking tray with plastic wrap or cellophane, ensuring it is free from creases. Spread with 100 g (3¹/2 oz) melted dark chocolate in a thin layer. Allow to set, then break into pieces and use to decorate desserts or the sides of cakes. Before the chocolate sets, you can sprinkle it with small pieces of nuts or crushed honeycomb, or apply tiny pieces of gold leaf after the chocolate has set.

～ Hot Chocolate Soufflés ～

Preparation time:
30 minutes
Total cooking time:
20 minutes
Serves 6

---

175 g (6 oz) dark
  chocolate, chopped
1/4 cup (60 ml/2 fl oz)
  Cointreau
5 egg yolks, lightly
  beaten
1/4 cup (60 g/2 oz)
  caster sugar
7 egg whites
icing sugar, to dust

---

1 Preheat the oven to moderately hot 200°C (400°F/Gas 6). Brush six 1 cup (250 ml/ 8 fl oz) ramekins well with melted butter. Wrap a double layer of baking paper around the dishes, coming about 3 cm (1¹/4 inches) above the top of the dishes. Secure with string and place on a baking tray.
2 Put the chocolate in a heatproof bowl. Half fill a saucepan with water and bring to the boil. Remove from the heat and place the bowl over the pan, making sure it is not touching the water. Stir occasionally until the chocolate is melted. Whisk in the Cointreau until well combined. Stir in the egg yolks and sugar. Transfer the mixture to a large mixing bowl.
3 Beat the egg whites in a large bowl with an electric mixer until firm peaks form. Fold a third of the beaten egg whites through the chocolate mixture. Using a metal spoon, fold in the remainder of the egg white until the mixture is just combined.

4 Spoon the mixture into the ramekins and run your thumb around the inside edge of each filled dish to ensure that the soufflés rise evenly. Bake for 12–15 minutes, or until the soufflés are well risen and have just set. Do not open the oven before the shortest cooking time has passed, or the soufflés will collapse. Cut the string and remove the collars from the soufflé dishes. Serve immediately, dusted lightly with the sifted icing sugar.

NUTRITION PER SERVE
Protein 8 g; Fat 10 g; Carbohydrate 35 g; Dietary Fibre 0 g; Cholesterol 150 mg; 1230 kJ (295 cal)

Variation Cut a hole in the centre of the cooked soufflés and drop in a spoonful of thick cream.

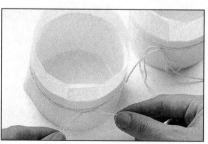

Wrap a double layer of baking paper around the ramekins and tie with string.

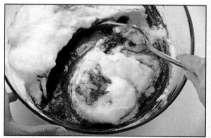

Fold the remaining egg white through the chocolate mixture.

~ Devil's Food Cake ~

Preparation time:
30 minutes
Total cooking time:
55 minutes
Serves 8

1½ cups (345 g/11 oz)
  firmly packed soft
  brown sugar
⅓ cup (40 g/1¼ oz)
  cocoa powder
1 cup (250 ml/8 fl oz)
  milk
90 g (3 oz) dark
  chocolate, chopped
125 g (4 oz) butter
1 teaspoon vanilla
  essence
2 eggs, separated
1½ cups (185 g/6 oz)
  plain flour

1 teaspoon bicarbonate
  of soda

Chocolate Icing
50 g (1¾ oz) dark
  chocolate, chopped
30 g (1 oz) butter
1 tablespoon icing sugar

Filling
1 cup (250 ml/8 fl oz)
  cream
1 tablespoon icing sugar
1 teaspoon vanilla
  essence

1 ~ Preheat the oven to warm 160°C (315°F/ Gas 2–3). Lightly grease two deep 20 cm (8 inch) round cake tins, and line the bases with baking paper. Combine a third of the brown sugar with the cocoa and milk in a small pan. Stir over low heat until the sugar and cocoa have dissolved. Remove from the heat and stir in the chocolate, stirring until it is melted. Allow to cool.
2 ~ Cream the remaining brown sugar with the butter and vanilla in a small bowl with an electric mixer until the mixture is light and fluffy. Beat in the egg yolks and the cooled chocolate mixture. Transfer the mixture to a large bowl, and stir in the sifted flour and bicarbonate of soda.
3 ~ Beat the egg whites in a small bowl until soft peaks form. Fold into the chocolate mixture. Divide the mixture evenly between the tins.

Bake for 35 minutes, or until a skewer inserted into the centre of the cakes comes out clean. Leave the cakes in the tins for 5 minutes before turning them out onto a wire rack to cool.
4 ~ To make the icing, put the chocolate and butter in a heatproof bowl. Place the bowl over a pan of simmering water, making sure it does not touch the water, and stir until the mixture is melted and smooth. Gradually add the sifted icing sugar and stir until smooth.
5 ~ To make the filling, whip the cream, icing sugar and vanilla in a small bowl with an electric mixer until stiff peaks form.

6 ~ Spread the filling over one of the cold cakes. Top with the second cake and spread the icing over the top. Decorate with chocolate curls (see page 55).

NUTRITION PER SERVE
Protein 8 g; Fat 35 g;
Carbohydrate 80 g; Dietary
Fibre 1 g; Cholesterol 130 mg;
2645 kJ (630 cal)

Note ~ Devil's Food Cake is a dark, dense chocolate cake, made with lots of chocolate, butter and eggs, and usually filled with whipped cream. At the other end of the spectrum is the light, airy Angel's Food Cake, made without fat. Both cakes are very popular in America.

Lightly grease the cake tins and cover the bases with baking paper.

Bake the cakes until a skewer inserted into the centre comes out clean.

～ Frozen Chocolate Parfait ～

Preparation time:
40 minutes
+ overnight freezing
Total cooking time:
25 minutes
Serves 8

6 egg yolks
1/2 cup (125 g/4 oz)
  caster sugar
150 g (5 oz) dark
  chocolate, finely
  chopped
150 g (5 oz) milk
  chocolate, finely
  chopped

1 cup (250 ml/8 fl oz)
  milk
1 vanilla pod, split
  lengthways
1 1/3 cups (350 ml/
  11 fl oz) cream

1. Lightly grease a 14 x 21 cm (5 1/2 x 8 1/2 inch) loaf pan and line with layers of plastic wrap or freezer wrap, allowing the plastic to come over the sides. (This will help when removing the parfait once it has set.)
2. Place the egg yolks in a bowl and gradually whisk in the sugar. Continue to whisk until the sugar has dissolved and the mixture is light and creamy. (Do not use an electric mixer as this will incorporate too much air into the mixture.) Place the chopped dark and milk chocolate in separate bowls and set aside.
3. Place the milk in a small pan. Scrape the seeds from the vanilla pod into the pan and add the pod. Slowly bring to the boil, then remove from the heat and remove the vanilla pod. Pour the hot milk onto the egg yolks, whisking constantly. Return the mixture to a clean pan and cook over low heat, stirring constantly, until the custard coats the back of a wooden spoon. This will take about 20 minutes. Do not overcook or the egg yolks will curdle.
4. Divide the hot custard evenly between the bowls of dark and milk chocolate. Using a wooden spoon, quickly mix in the custard, stirring until the chocolate is completely melted. Allow to cool completely. Beat the cream with electric beaters until soft peaks form. Divide evenly between the cooled chocolate mixtures, and gently fold in.
5. Carefully pour the dark chocolate mixture into the tin. Freeze for 30 minutes, or until the dark chocolate is firm. Pour the milk chocolate mixture over the frozen dark chocolate to form an even layer, and smooth the top with the back of a spoon. Cover and freeze overnight, or until the parfait is completely frozen.
6. Just before serving, carefully remove the parfait from the tin with the plastic wrap. Remove the plastic wrap. Slice the parfait and serve immediately, returning the remaining portion to the freezer. Delicious served with fresh berries.

NUTRITION PER SERVE
Protein 5 g; Fat 30 g;
Carbohydrate 30 g; Dietary
Fibre 0 g; Cholesterol 200 mg;
1685 kJ (400 cal)

Note If you have trouble removing the parfait from the tin, quickly run a warm wet cloth around the outside of the tin to loosen the parfait.

Divide the hot custard evenly between the bowls of dark and milk chocolate.

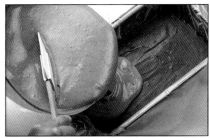

Pour the milk chocolate mixture over the frozen dark chocolate layer.

~ Chocolate Fondue Platter ~

Preparation time:
30 minutes
Total cooking time:
20 minutes
Serves 6–8

marshmallows and
chopped fruit, to serve

Dark Chocolate Fondue
**250 g (8 oz) dark
chocolate, chopped**
**$1/2$ cup (125 ml/4 fl oz)
thick cream**
**2–3 teaspoons
Cointreau**

*White Chocolate
Fondue*
**$2/3$ cup (170 ml/5$1/2$ fl oz)
thick cream**
**$1/2$ cup (125 ml/4 fl oz)
light corn syrup**
**$1/4$ cup (60 ml/2 fl oz)
Cointreau**
**250 g (8 oz) white
chocolate bits**

1 ~ To make the dark chocolate fondue, put the chocolate and cream in a heatproof bowl. Stand the bowl over a pan of simmering water. Stir until smooth. Remove from the heat and stir in the Cointreau.
2 ~ To make the white chocolate fondue, combine the cream and corn syrup in a small pan. Bring to the boil, then remove from the heat. Add the Cointreau and white chocolate. Stir until melted and smooth.

Serve with the marshmallows and fruit.

NUTRITION PER SERVE (8)
Protein 5 g; Fat 35 g; Carbohydrate 60 g; Dietary Fibre 1 g; Cholesterol 60 mg; 2335 kJ (560 cal)

Put the dark chocolate and cream in a heatproof bowl over simmering water.

Remove the chocolate mixture from the heat and stir in the Cointreau.

Combine the cream and corn syrup in a small pan.

Remove the pan from the heat and stir in the Cointreau and white chocolate.

～ Index ～

Front cover: Baked Chocolate Cheesecake; Chocolate-coffee Cups; Chocolate Clusters; and Moist Chocolate Brownies.